REFLECTIONS
FOR
ADVENT

30 November – 24 December 2015

MAGGI DAWN
BARBARA MOSSE

with an introduction to Advent
by SAMUEL WELLS

Church House Publishing
Church House
Great Smith Street
London SW1P 3AZ

ISBN 978 0 7151 4690 3

Published 2015 by Church House Publishing
Copyright © The Archbishops' Council 2015

The opinions expressed in this book are those of the
authors and do not necessarily reflect the official policy
of the General Synod or The Archbishops' Council of the
Church of England.

Liturgical editor: Peter Moger
Series editor: Hugh Hillyard-Parker
Designed and typeset by Hugh Hillyard-Parker
Copy edited by: Ros Connelly
Printed by Ashford Colour Press Ltd., Gosport, Hampshire

What do you think of *Reflections for Daily Prayer*?

We'd love to hear from you – simply email us at

publishing@churchofengland.org

or write to us at

Church House Publishing, Church House,
Great Smith Street, London SW1P 3AZ.

Visit **www.dailyprayer.org.uk** for more
information on the *Reflections* series, ordering
and subscriptions.

Contents

About *Reflections for Advent*

Based on the *Common Worship Lectionary* readings for Morning Prayer, these daily reflections are designed to refresh and inspire times of personal prayer. The aim is to provide rich, contemporary and engaging insights into Scripture.

Each page lists the Lectionary readings for the day, with the main psalms for that day highlighted in **bold**. The Collect of the day – either the *Common Worship* collect or the shorter additional Collect – is also included.

For those using this book in conjunction with a service of Morning Prayer, the following conventions apply: a psalm printed in parentheses is omitted if it has been used as the opening canticle at that office; a psalm marked with an asterisk may be shortened if desired.

A short reflection is provided on either the Old or New Testament reading. Popular writers, experienced ministers, biblical scholars and theologians have contributed to this series, bringing their own emphases, enthusiasms and approaches to biblical interpretation to bear.

Regular users of Morning Prayer and *Time to Pray* (from *Common Worship: Daily Prayer*) and anyone who follows the Lectionary for their regular Bible reading will benefit from the rich variety of traditions represented in these stimulating and accessible pieces.

This volume also includes both a simple form of *Common Worship: Morning Prayer* (see pp. 32–3) and a short form of Night Prayer – also known as Compline – (see pp. 36–9), particularly for the benefit of those readers who are new to the habit of the Daily Office or for any reader while travelling.

1

About the authors

Maggi Dawn is Associate Professor of Theology and Literature, and Dean of Marquand Chapel, at Yale Divinity School in the USA. Trained in both music and theology, her publications include five albums of songs, five books, and numerous articles and chapters. She was ordained in the Diocese of Ely, and holds a PhD from the University of Cambridge.

Barbara Mosse is a writer and retired Anglican priest. Prior to retirement she was a lecturer on the MA in Christian Spirituality at Sarum College, Salisbury. Earlier ministerial posts included some parish work, alongside chaplaincy experience in prison, university, community mental health and hospital. She is the author of *The Treasures of Darkness, Encircling the Christian Year* and *Welcoming the Way of the Cross*.

Stephen Cottrell is the Bishop of Chelmsford. Before this he was Bishop of Reading and has worked in parishes in London, Chichester, and Huddersfield and as Pastor of Peterborough Cathedral. He is a well-known writer and speaker on evangelism, spirituality and catechesis. His best-selling *How to Pray* (CHP) and *How to Live* (CHP) have recently been reissued.

John Pritchard has recently retired as Bishop of Oxford. Prior to that he has been Bishop of Jarrow, Archdeacon of Canterbury and Warden of Cranmer Hall, Durham. His only ambition was to be a vicar, which he was in Taunton for eight happy years. He enjoys armchair sport, walking, reading, music, theatre and recovering.

Samuel Wells is Vicar of St Martin in the Fields, London, and Visiting Professor of Christian Ethics at King's College, London. He is the author of a number of acclaimed books; his most recent titles are *What Anglicans Believe, Crafting Prayers for Public Worship* and *Learning to Dream Again*. He was formerly Dean of the Chapel and Research Professor of Christian Ethics at Duke University, North Carolina.

'Never Mind the Width ...'
– A reflection on the season of Advent

Back in the days when it was common to go into a tailor's shop and ask for yards of cloth for sewing or dressmaking into trousers or skirts or outer garments, people would imitate the proverbial salesperson and say, 'Never mind the quality – feel the width!' In other words, 'Who cares whether the material is the very best fabric? See how much there is of it, for such a bargain price!' It's a parable for what we do to our lives to hide ourselves from the depths of our struggles and sadness and pain. 'Never mind our deepest desires – see how easy it is to occupy ourselves with our most trivial ones! Don't distress yourself about the things that really matter – see how quickly you can get your hands on the things that don't!' It's perfectly possible to turn your whole life into a distraction, a whole enterprise of feeling the width. Maybe that's what you're doing right now.

The Church has a season for helping us set aside our distractions and get profoundly in touch with the powerlessness of waiting. It's called Advent. In Advent we dismantle our elaborate defences, and, for a few weeks, or days, or moments, face up squarely to our deepest yearnings, our unresolved longings and our rawest needs. But Advent is also about a confidence deeper than our needs, a hope more far-reaching than our desires, a future more comprehensive than our most poignant yearnings.

In our self-protection we habitually say to ourselves, to one another, and even to God, 'Never mind the quality, feel the width. Let's just make ourselves busy and perhaps we'll forget about all the tricky stuff.' In Advent, God says to us, 'Never mind the width. Your life isn't about quantity of activity or length of days. Let go of the width. Feel the depth.'

The answer to the agony of waiting isn't width. It's depth. Just for once, in this Advent season, feel the depth of your life, and look into the deep heart of God. Look at your hands. Think of the Father's hands that made the world; think of the Son's hands and the nail-marks in the centre of them; think of the Spirit's hands, and realize they're the hands you're looking at right now. Look at your feet. These are feet that can walk with others in their pain; these are feet that can dance to the beat of God's heart; these are feet that can run with the wind of God's Spirit.

3

Feel your skin. Skin that Christ took on; skin that can touch the tender suffering of another; skin that's made to protect and stretch the boundary of your being. Feel the depth.

Advent says, 'Yes, you're hungry. Yes, you long for fulfilment and resolution and completion and consummation. Yes, you're aching all over; yes, if you stopped your incessant activity and paused for one second to look in the mirror, you'd be sobbing with disappointed dreams and deflated desires and unmet longings and dashed aspirations. Yes, life hasn't turned out as you trusted it would; yes, it feels like everyone else has it easier than you; yes, it's sometimes impossible to find the patience to keep going; yes, you feel that if for one moment you admitted your grief, it would crush you and incapacitate you and disable you from functioning in any respectable and grown-up way.' Advent gets to the bottom of our waiting.

But Advent doesn't stop there. Advent goes under and around our waiting. Advent also says, gently, cherishingly and tenderly, 'No. No, this isn't the way the story ends. No, God isn't ignoring you or punishing you. No, this isn't God's last word on the matter. No, God hasn't finished with you. No, this groaning, this aching, this yearning won't be your eternal condition. God came in Christ to be with you, to groan with your groaning, to ache with your aching, to yearn with your yearning. God in Christ suffered on the cross to show you a yearning that is greater even than your yearning, a grieving that is greater even than your grieving, a longing that is greater even than your longing. A yearning and a longing *for you*. Christ rose from the dead to show you how the story ends, that all your pain and agony and tears will be taken up into glory, that all your sadness will be made beautiful and all your waiting will be rewarded. Christ ascended into heaven to show you that you'll spend eternity with God, that your hunger will be met in God's banquet, that everything you long for will be exceeded and overwhelmed in the glory of the presence of God, and that when you see the marks in Christ's hands and the Father's broken heart, you'll finally realize how achingly, convulsingly hungry God has always been for you.'

Just for once this Advent, dare to feel the depth. Never mind the width. If you're tired of waiting, go deeper. Feel the deep texture of life. Eternal life isn't an infinitely extended version of what we have now: it's a deeper version of what we have now. If you want a glimpse of eternal life, even amid the sadness and the longing of waiting, go deeper.

Remember all those people you were envious of and who seemed to have everything you didn't have? Go deeper and see who they really are and what they truly long for, and feel your jealousy begin to melt into compassion. Go deeper into your fears and come out of the bottom of them, and let your hatred become hope. Go deeper into your loneliness and make a companion of the truth you find there. Feel the wonder of your createdness, sense the unlikely mystery of your being here at all. And receive all the rest as a bonus, a gift, a blessing.

Advent isn't an escape. It's an encounter with the time that's deeper than our time, a time we call eternal life. It's a discovery of a longing that's deeper than our longing, the longing we call God's waiting for us. It's an experience deep down and, through the bottom of our experience, a place where grief is no longer isolating but companionable, where alienating hurt becomes tender wisdom, where unfulfilled longing becomes the sculpting of a greater hole for grace.

It's hard to do Advent all year round. It's almost easier to be left alone in our waiting. But just this once, this Advent, take the risk on God that God's taken on you. Feel the quality. Feel the depth. Go deeper and keep digging. Keep digging until you find you've dug deep into the heart of God.

Samuel Wells

The importance of daily prayer

Daily prayer is a way of sustaining that most special of all relationships. It helps if we want to pray, but it can be sufficient to want to want to pray, or even to want to want to want to pray! The direction of the heart is what matters, not its achievements. Gradually we are shaped and changed by the practice of daily prayer. Apprentices in prayer never graduate, but we become a little bit more the people God wants us to be.

Prayer isn't a technique; it's a relationship, and it starts in the most ordinary, instinctive reactions to everyday life:

- **Gratitude**: good things are always happening to us, however small.
- **Wonder**: we often see amazing things in nature and in people but pass them by.
- **Need**: we bump into scores of needs every day.
- **Sorrow**: we mess up.

Prayer is taking those instincts and stretching them out before God. The rules then are: start small, stay natural, be honest.

Here are four ways of putting some structure around daily prayer.

1 **The Quiet Time**. This is the classic way of reading a passage of the Bible, using Bible reading reflections like those in this book, and then praying naturally about the way the passage has struck you, taking to God the questions, resolutions, hopes, fears and other responses that have arisen within you.

2 **The Daily Office**. This is a structured way of reading Scripture and psalms, and praying for individuals, the world, the day ahead, etc. It keeps us anchored in the Lectionary, the basic reading of the Church, and so ensures that we engage with the breadth of Scripture, rather than just with our favourite passages. It also puts us in living touch with countless others around the world who are doing something similar. There is a simple form of Morning Prayer on pp. 32–3 and a form of Night Prayer (Compline) on pp. 36–9. Fuller forms can be found in *Common Worship: Daily Prayer*.

3   **Holy Reading**. Also known as *Lectio Divina*, this is a tried and trusted way of feeding and meditating on the Bible, described more fully on pages 8–9 of this book. In essence, here is how it is done:

- *Read:* Read the passage slowly until a phrase catches your attention.
- *Reflect:* Chew the phrase carefully, drawing the goodness out of it.
- *Respond:* Pray about the thoughts and feelings that have surfaced in you.
- *Rest:* You may want to rest in silence for a while.
- *Repeat:* Carry on with the passage ...

4   **Silence**. In our distracted culture some people are drawn more to silence than to words. This will involve *centring* (hunkering down), *focusing* on a short biblical phrase (such as 'Come, Holy Spirit'), *waiting* (repeating the phrase as necessary), and *ending* (perhaps with the Lord's Prayer). The length of time is irrelevant.

There are, of course, as many ways of praying as there are people to pray. There are no right or wrong ways to pray. 'Pray as you can, not as you can't', is wise advice. The most important thing is to make sure there is sufficient structure to keep prayer going when it's a struggle as well as when it's a joy. Prayer is too important to leave to chance.

+*John Pritchard*

Lectio Divina – a way of reading the Bible

Lectio Divina is a contemplative way of reading the Bible. It dates back to the early centuries of the Christian Church and was established as a monastic practice by Benedict in the sixth century. It is a way of praying the Scriptures that leads us deeper into God's word. We slow down. We read a short passage more than once. We chew it over slowly and carefully. We savour it. Scripture begins to speak to us in a new way. It speaks to us personally, and aids that union we have with God through Christ, who is himself the Living Word.

Make sure you are sitting comfortably. Breathe slowly and deeply. Ask God to speak to you through the passage that you are about to read.

This way of praying starts with our silence. We often make the mistake of thinking prayer is about what we say to God. It is actually the other way round. God wants to speak to us. He will do this through the Scriptures. So don't worry about what to say. Don't worry if nothing jumps out at you at first. God is patient. He will wait for the opportunity to get in. He will give you a word and lead you to understand its meaning for you today.

First reading: Listen

As you read the passage listen for a word or phrase that attracts you. Allow it to arise from the passage as if it is God's word for you today. Sit in silence repeating the word or phrase in your head.

Then say the word or phrase aloud.

Second reading: Ponder

As you read the passage again, ask how this word or phrase speaks to your life and why it has connected with you. Ponder it carefully. Don't worry if you get distracted – it may be part of your response to offer to God. Sit in silence and then frame a single sentence that begins to say aloud what this word or phrase says to you.

Third reading: Pray

As you read the passage for the last time, ask what Christ is calling from you. What is it that you need to do or consider or relinquish or take on as a result of what God is saying to you in this word or phrase? In the silence that follows the reading, pray for the grace of the Spirit to plant this word in your heart.

If you are in a group, talk for a few minutes and pray with each other.

If you are on your own, speak your prayer to God either aloud or in the silence of your heart.

If there is time, you may even want to read the passage a fourth time, and then end with the same silence before God with which you began.

+Stephen Cottrell

Monday 30 November
Andrew the Apostle

Psalms 47, 147.1-12
Ezekiel 47.1-12
or Ecclesiasticus 14.20-end
John 12.20-32

John 12.20-32

'... unless a grain of wheat falls into the earth and dies' (v.24)

In this first week of Advent, we celebrate another first: the first disciple to be called by Jesus. There were two pairs of brothers among the disciples: Andrew and Simon Peter, and James and John. Yet while three of these were especially close to Jesus, Andrew was often left out. Simon Peter is usually credited with being the first to confess that Jesus was the Messiah, yet according to John 1.41, Andrew perceived this at his first encounter with Jesus and he immediately told Simon. Both in this passage, and at the feeding of the 5,000, Andrew seems to act as a buffer between Jesus and the crowds. It seems that, like many personal assistants, he often worked tirelessly in the background while others got the glory.

Perhaps, being Simon Peter's younger brother, Andrew was used to living in someone else's shadow. Perhaps that made it easier for him, when he heard Jesus say 'unless a grain of wheat falls', not only to hear Jesus' prophetic words about his own death, but also to embrace their wider implications: that unless we are willing to lay down our small ambitions, we will never see or understand true glory. Real glory isn't about being in the spotlight all the time, but rather is about being transformed to reflect the glory of God. If that means sacrificing acknowledgement, or taking second place to someone else, it's a price worth paying.

COLLECT

Almighty God,
who gave such grace to your apostle Saint Andrew
that he readily obeyed the call of your Son Jesus Christ
    and brought his brother with him:
call us by your holy word,
and give us grace to follow you without delay
    and to tell the good news of your kingdom;
through Jesus Christ your Son our Lord,
who is alive and reigns with you,
in the unity of the Holy Spirit,
one God, now and for ever.

Psalms **80**, 82 *or* **5**, 6 (8)
Isaiah 26.1-13
Matthew 12.22-37

Isaiah 26.1-13

'... this song will be sung in the land of Judah
... the way of the righteous is level' (vv.1,7)

Isaiah often uses poetic metaphors to describe his vision of justice and equity. Here, high cities are brought low; in chapter 40, mountains and valleys are made level. But Isaiah not only speaks of justice; he frames it as a song to be sung, with similar themes to other justice songs sung by Deborah (Judges 5), Hannah (1 Samuel 2), and Mary (Luke 1), and the psalmists.

Songs have historically taken on an important role in situations where justice is nowhere to be found. We have songs as old as Psalm 137, and as recent as the spirituals of eighteenth- and nineteenth-century America, through which enslaved people expressed a depth of lament, a determination to survive, and a refusal to lose their human dignity. Or think of protest songs: *The Diggers Song* is famed as a seventeenth-century protest song over land rights; *We Shall Overcome* was the anthem of the labour and civil rights movements, and later a song of anti-war protest. During the years of apartheid in South Africa, resistance music was often described as a 'weapon of struggle'.

Songs can be tools of protest and change, etching on the heart the Advent longing for the world as it should be. As Isaiah calls on God to level out mountain-sized inequities, he also recognizes that a world in need of justice is a world in need of songs to sustain the soul.

Almighty God,
give us grace to cast away the works of darkness
and to put on the armour of light,
now in the time of this mortal life,
in which your Son Jesus Christ came to us in great humility;
that on the last day,
when he shall come again in his glorious majesty
to judge the living and the dead,
we may rise to the life immortal;
through him who is alive and reigns with you,
in the unity of the Holy Spirit,
one God, now and for ever.

COLLECT

11

Wednesday 2 December

Psalms 5, **7** *or* **119.1-32**
Isaiah 28.1-13
Matthew 12.38-end

Isaiah 28.1-13

'... like a first-ripe fig before the summer' (v.4)

For Ephraim, as now, figs were really a summer crop. But a few small, early figs would appear in the spring, and these were a particularly fine delicacy. Ephraim (another name for the Northern Kingdom of Israel) was a well-developed culture, a wealthy and stable society. But Isaiah saw what is true of many an empire just before its fall: a society resting on its laurels, so confident in its history and traditions that it believes nothing can assail it. Ephraim's complacency made her vulnerable to being snatched like an early fig, and 'eaten alive' by approaching enemy armies.

Just as the over-satisfied feeling after a big meal makes you want to take a little nap, so Isaiah laments that his people are so self-satisfied with their status and tradition that they cannot hear the need for change or the call to action. For cultures with a long and secure history, it seems impossible to imagine that old and beautiful buildings, ancient institutions or venerated practices might not be there forever. A sense of 'rightness' about their existence can lead to poor investments and unstable alliances, for the sake of preserving things as they are. For Isaiah's readers, the consequences were devastating. For us, too, it is important to avoid complacency about what we take for granted; our own institutions and long-held traditions may not be as solid and impermeable as we would like to believe.

COLLECT

Almighty God,
give us grace to cast away the works of darkness
and to put on the armour of light,
now in the time of this mortal life,
in which your Son Jesus Christ came to us in great humility;
that on the last day,
when he shall come again in his glorious majesty
    to judge the living and the dead,
we may rise to the life immortal;
through him who is alive and reigns with you,
in the unity of the Holy Spirit,
one God, now and for ever.

Psalms **42**, 43 *or* 14, **15**, 16
Isaiah 28.14-end
Matthew 13.1-23

Isaiah 28.14-end

'Therefore hear the word of the Lord, you scoffers' (v.14)

This short passage compares the health of society with the workmanship in a building. Just as a building is measured and tested with a line and plummet, so justice and righteousness are the qualities by which society is measured. Whatever is not properly constructed, whatever lacks a cornerstone, will be swept away by storms, and only what is upright and true will stand.

But what strikes me is that it is addressed to 'you scoffers'. Scoffing is a mode of speech that shuts down dialogue; it cuts the ground from under the feet of another person who could have been a conversation partner but instead is silenced. Life-giving conversation comes from listening, talking, considering, adjusting our viewpoint in the light of what we learn. But a scoffer is disdainful, supercilious, dismissive, someone who judges prematurely and assumes a place of superiority. Brushing off another's point of view with cruel humour may make the scoffer look 'cool' or funny, but scoffing isolates a person from friends and community, suffocating relationships and driving away goodwill.

Dialogue can open people up or shut them down, and Isaiah put his finger on what makes the difference: it is not just the content, but the spirit of conversation that makes it life-giving or deadening. The scoffers he addressed may even have been intellectually brilliant, but they brought such a negative spirit to their conversation that they had made a kind of 'covenant with death' (v.15).

Almighty God,
as your kingdom dawns,
turn us from the darkness of sin to the light of holiness,
that we may be ready to meet you
in our Lord and Saviour, Jesus Christ.

COLLECT

13

Friday 4 December

Isaiah 29.1-14

'… their worship of me is a human commandment learned by rote'
(v.13)

Isaiah's challenge may sound alarming to a liturgical community. When we revisit the same themes Advent after Advent, or if we daily recite the same words, learned by rote or read from a book, are our hearts far from God? Working in an ecumenical setting, I frequently hear debates between members of my congregation as to the relative value of liturgical and extempore styles of worship. Is one more heartfelt than the other? Is it more sincere to write prayers in advance, or to speak spontaneously in the moment?

Listen closely to extempore prayer, though, and you will see that it is just as much a learned and repeated pattern as liturgical worship, with language so particular to each community that you can even tell quite accurately which denomination a prayer comes from – Baptist or Pentecostal, Hillsong, Vineyard, or New Wine.

Whatever the style, repeating patterns of worship can either inoculate us against God's spirit, or cut a deep groove in our hearts. We can recite words while our hearts are disengaged, or we can discover ever-deeper layers of truth as we worship. Isaiah was not distinguishing between genres of prayer, but asking whether the community offered their prayer from the heart. Doing religion for the sake of it is worse than not doing it at all. Whatever the style, what matters is whether we are searching for God as we voice our songs and prayers in worship.

COLLECT

Almighty God,
give us grace to cast away the works of darkness
and to put on the armour of light,
now in the time of this mortal life,
in which your Son Jesus Christ came to us in great humility;
that on the last day,
when he shall come again in his glorious majesty
    to judge the living and the dead,
we may rise to the life immortal;
through him who is alive and reigns with you,
in the unity of the Holy Spirit,
one God, now and for ever.

Psalms **9**, (10) *or* 20, 21, **23**
Isaiah 29.15-end
Matthew 13.44-end

Isaiah 29.15-end

'You turn things upside down!' (v.16)

The World Turned Upside Down was a famous English broadside ballad, published in the mid 1640s. It was written as a protest song against the attempts of the government to make Christmas a more solemn and sober occasion. At the time, Advent gave way to nearly two weeks of Christmas celebrations that continued until early January, during which time there was a ritualized reversal of social norms known as 'misrule'. Presided over by a Lord of Misrule, a child would be made Bishop for a day, masters waited upon their servants, and for a short time the world really was turned upside down. Some historians claim this provided a necessary release of tensions in seventeenth-century English society. However, a puritan faction within the government, shocked by the immoral behaviour that accompanied the celebrations, attempted to outlaw the tradition and make Christmas more 'Christ-like'.

It's easy to mistake Isaiah's call to righteousness for this kind of puritanical demand for personal holiness. But his longing for redemption was more in the spirit of Advent – less concerned with deliverance from personal sin than from systemic evil, when 'the tyrant shall be no more' (v.20). The tradition of misrule was a reminder of – and in some sense a protest against – social inequity and the abuse of power. Like the Lord of Misrule, Isaiah called for radical social and political change, and a reversal of power relationships, to turn the world right-side-up.

Almighty God,
as your kingdom dawns,
turn us from the darkness of sin to the light of holiness,
that we may be ready to meet you
in our Lord and Saviour, Jesus Christ.

COLLECT

15

Monday 7 December

Isaiah 30.1-18

'Go now, write it before them on a tablet, and inscribe it in a book ...' (v.8)

Engraved into stone, pressed into clay, painted on ceramic, tooled into wax or inked onto animal skin, the written word was well developed by Isaiah's time, and has ever since had a quality of permanence. Every technological development in the production of writing has changed the way we relate to text; every change has caused alarm as well as excitement at the never-ending possibilities of speaking, reading and writing words. In the fifteenth century, the Gutenberg press led to silent reading overtaking reading aloud; later, the paperback reduced the sense of reverence for books. Turning print to pixels not only made words searchable, it changed the way we engage with text. Words on the web are more permanent than ever before, yet seem more ephemeral; they combine the visual with the aural; they have morphed from the linear arguments of traditional books to an interactive, networked engagement with words.

Isaiah captures one of the difficulties of language: that it is both our best means of communication, and at the same time always inadequate to the task. Words can weave 'illusions' (v.10) that conceal the truth, or they can take us closer to it. Perhaps it is no mistake that one of our names for Christ is 'the Word' – for in the end meaning resides neither in speech, print, nor pixels; our relationship to words constantly changes, but our faith is not ultimately anchored to words, but to *the* Word.

COLLECT

O Lord, raise up, we pray, your power
and come among us,
and with great might succour us;
that whereas, through our sins and wickedness
we are grievously hindered
in running the race that is set before us,
your bountiful grace and mercy
may speedily help and deliver us;
through Jesus Christ your Son our Lord,
to whom with you and the Holy Spirit,
be honour and glory, now and for ever.

Psalms **56**, 57 *or* 32, **36**
Isaiah 30.19-end
Matthew 14.13-end

Isaiah 30.19-end

'This is the way; walk in it.' (v.21)

For people of faith, taking care over decisions is a regular preoccupation, either in terms of the ethical obligations and consequences of faith, or with a more specific notion of God's personal guidance.

There might seem to be an immediate correlation between the importance of a particular decision and how much time it takes to make it. But life is not so simple. Sometimes we have the luxury of time, and a decision may be deferred until the way becomes certain, while at other times, even with a weighty matter, the right decision may be crystal clear in an instant. Far more complicated are those paralyzing moments when an urgent decision is required, but it is still unclear which way to go.

Someone once said to me that you can only steer a moving ship. When we don't know what to do, sometimes the moment of clarity about which way to go doesn't come while we are pausing and pondering. It may be that the direction will only become clear to see once we are actually on the move. Sometimes, rather than asking which way to go, we simply need to get started, trusting that the direction will become clear as we take the first steps: '... when you turn to the right or when you turn to the left, your ears shall hear a word behind you, saying, "This is the way; walk in it".' (v.21)

Almighty God,
purify our hearts and minds,
that when your Son Jesus Christ comes again as
judge and saviour
we may be ready to receive him,
who is our Lord and our God.

COLLECT

Wednesday 9 December

Isaiah 31

'[the Lord] … does not call back his words' (v.2)

A linguistic dichotomy between fluid, poetic meanings and stable meanings is constantly in play in the words of Scripture. Studies over recent decades have opened up our understanding of the uses of language – how what is said is inflected in the way it is said; how form and content are woven together to make meaning; how some modes of language are wide open for interpretation, while the meaning of others are more tightly understood. 'We look for His coming again' begins a discussion with never-ending ramifications, but 'I will' is not only clear in its intent, but is a vow that actually changes one's status.

Isaiah reminds us of the danger of treating God as a malleable concept that we can interpret at will. God's words are not 'called back'; God does not break vows, or cheapen promises. Stable meaning, though, does not imply stasis or immovability; rather it recognizes the power of words to make something happen. Isaiah develops the theme in 55.11: 'my word … that goes out from my mouth … shall not return to me empty, but … succeed in the thing for which I sent it.' A promise or a vow is a creative force that makes something happen; it has active power to bring into being what was not there before. This is supremely true of God's words, but it is true of our words also: kept promises have the creative power to change our world.

COLLECT

O Lord, raise up, we pray, your power
and come among us,
and with great might succour us;
that whereas, through our sins and wickedness
we are grievously hindered
in running the race that is set before us,
your bountiful grace and mercy
may speedily help and deliver us;
through Jesus Christ your Son our Lord,
to whom with you and the Holy Spirit,
be honour and glory, now and for ever.

Psalms 53, **54**, 60 *or* **37***
Isaiah 32
Matthew 15.21-28

Isaiah 32

'The effect of righteousness will be peace' (v.17)

'Righteousness' is a frame for this passage, which begins with a prediction of God's righteous reign and ends with a description of life in a society built on righteousness. In current parlance, 'righteousness' has rather negative overtones, summoning up the unattractive image of a holier-than-thou, self-righteous person who preaches arbitrary, restrictive rules. For Isaiah, however, righteousness is not about refraining from a list of randomly forbidden activities, but ordering society rightly with fairness and equity such that justice and peace prevail. Righteousness is active, not passive; strong, not weak.

The sense of this reading is summed up well in the often-quoted maxim of political theorist and philosopher Edmund Burke: 'The only thing necessary for the triumph of evil is for good men to do nothing.' Burke, in eighteenth-century vernacular, addressed his maxim to men, and it is often said that we should assume this included women. It is doubly interesting, then, that some two and a half millennia earlier, Isaiah regularly made a point of addressing his prophecies specifically to women, demanding the same rigorous response from them as he did from men: 'Rise up, you women who are at ease, hear my voice; you complacent daughters, listen to my speech' (v.9). Isaiah expected women to be equally responsible for their destiny, giving them as much agency as men in whether or not they will choose righteousness and usher in God's reign.

Almighty God,
purify our hearts and minds,
that when your Son Jesus Christ comes again as
judge and saviour
we may be ready to receive him,
who is our Lord and our God.

COLLECT

Advent

Psalms 85, **86** *or* **31**
Isaiah 33.1-22
Matthew 15.29-end

Isaiah 33.1-22

'Lebanon is confounded and withers away; Sharon is like a desert' (v.9)

We often read Isaiah during Advent because he gives concrete meaning to redemption. Looking for Christ's second coming can seem disconnected from the real world, but Isaiah placed redemption in the immediate future. In predicting that the nation's immorality and spiritual unfaithfulness would be their downfall, he never divided spiritual matters from social, political or ecological issues.

His message is laced through with poetic imagery; he likens the coming disaster not only to pests destroying a harvest, but also to more comprehensive natural disasters resulting in the land withering and drying up. Sharon was an extremely fertile plain, a place of forests, flowers and lush vegetation; it must have seemed unimaginable that it could become a desert. Lebanon was famous for its beautiful cypress trees, for forests of cedars that were used in construction and shipbuilding, and for its vineyards. Could Lebanon really wither away? It is hard to tell whether Isaiah meant this poetically or literally, but more than two millennia later his words have a particular poignancy as we see devastating pollution, rapid extinction of species, severe droughts and melting ice caps, all resulting from industrial and natural disasters.

We urgently need to understand that the call to righteousness applies just as much to our relationship to the earth as it does to social relationships. The direct result of unrighteousness is not just that society fragments, but that the land itself mourns and languishes.

COLLECT

O Lord, raise up, we pray, your power
and come among us,
and with great might succour us;
that whereas, through our sins and wickedness
we are grievously hindered
in running the race that is set before us,
your bountiful grace and mercy
may speedily help and deliver us;
through Jesus Christ your Son our Lord,
to whom with you and the Holy Spirit,
be honour and glory, now and for ever.

20

Psalms **145** *or* 41, **42**, 43
Isaiah 35
Matthew 16.1-12

Isaiah 35

'A highway shall be there, and it shall be called the Holy Way' (v.8)

To modern ears, a highway in the desert may not sound like good news. We are glad of motorways when we need to get somewhere, but if you have ever crawled round the M25 on a Friday afternoon or languished in gridlocked highways around Los Angeles, a highway in the desert is the stuff of nightmares.

What did Isaiah have in mind? Not all the exiles returned to Judah, but first a large group, and later some smaller groups really did walk some 800 miles home through the desert to Jerusalem. In contrast to the 40 years of the Exodus, with their circuitous desert wanderings, Isaiah paints a picture of a safe, straight way home, where the withering of the land we read about yesterday (Isaiah 33.9) is reversed. It is a way through the desert laid about with oases of water to save them from the confusion of mirage and the beating sun; an immense pilgrimage on which no traveller would go astray; a road along which they would sing all the way home.

Troubled neither by the standstill of gridlock nor by wandering around in circles, the road home after a long, lonely exile is a way forward not backwards, a way towards a future and a hope, a way towards re-discovered identity and recovered dignity. This is the Holy Way, the highway God makes in the desert.

Almighty God,
purify our hearts and minds,
that when your Son Jesus Christ comes again as
judge and saviour
we may be ready to receive him,
who is our Lord and our God.

COLLECT

Monday 14 December

Psalm **40** *or* **44**
Isaiah 38.1-8, 21-22
Matthew 16.13-end

Isaiah 38.1-8, 21-22

'Set your house in order, for you shall die' (v.1)

Prophetic utterances make up much of the book of Isaiah. All prophecy arises from within a historical context, and prophecy does indeed play a part in today's reading, although it is set here within a wider account of a historical event. The cities of Judah have come under intense attack from the Assyrians, and in the midst of the crisis, the Judean king, Hezekiah, falls mortally ill. Although he does eventually recover, his septic boil being cured by the application of 'a lump of figs' (v.21), the Lord's initial prophecy through Isaiah is that the king will die and that he should prepare himself for death.

As we enter the third week of Advent, Isaiah's blunt message in verse 1 reminds us of the traditional Advent themes of death, judgement, hell and heaven (the 'four last things'). And the challenge is as relevant for us today as it was for Hezekiah: we may not die today, or tomorrow, next week or next year – but nothing in life is more certain than the fact that we *will* die, one day. One of Jesus' parables tells of a rich man whose energies were completely focused on the need for adequate storage for his crops, and his plans for a future life of ease (Luke 12.16-21). God calls him a fool and warns the man of his imminent death, shockingly reminding him of his mortality (Luke 12.20). The season of Advent offers us, too, such a bracing reminder.

COLLECT

O Lord Jesus Christ,
who at your first coming sent your messenger
to prepare your way before you:
grant that the ministers and stewards of your mysteries
may likewise so prepare and make ready your way
by turning the hearts of the disobedient to the wisdom of the just,
that at your second coming to judge the world
we may be found an acceptable people in your sight;
for you are alive and reign with the Father
in the unity of the Holy Spirit,
one God, now and for ever.

Tuesday 15 December

Isaiah 38.9-20

'O Lord, I am oppressed; be my security!' (v.14)

Despite the statement in verse 9, it is clear from the sentiments in this writing of Hezekiah that he had not, at this stage, recovered from his illness. He is writing from a very dark place and he believes he is dying (vv.10-11). The mood is reminiscent of a number of the psalms, such as Psalm 69 ('Save me, O God ... I sink in deep mire, where there is no foothold', vv.1,2), and of the response of Job to his unjust suffering ('Truly the thing that I fear comes upon me, and what I dread befalls me', Job 3.25).

Passages such as this one present a challenge to the modern reader. Hezekiah shares with the rest of the Israelite community the belief that God himself is the agent of illness and suffering (vv.13,15), and elsewhere in the Old Testament a link is explicitly made between illness and human sin (Deuteronomy 28.58-61). In its crude form, this is not a link that present-day Christianity would make. When healing a man born blind, Jesus repudiated his disciples' assumption that the man's affliction was God's punishment for sin, although he did also state that the man's blindness served God's purposes in other mysterious ways: 'Neither this man nor his parents sinned; he was born blind so that God's works might be revealed in him' (John 9.3).

This passage from Isaiah raises some profound questions, which Christians have wrestled with for generations. Does God intervene in human lives? Does he answer prayer – and if so, in what ways?

God for whom we watch and wait,
you sent John the Baptist to prepare the way of your Son:
give us courage to speak the truth,
to hunger for justice,
and to suffer for the cause of right,
with Jesus Christ our Lord.

COLLECT

Wednesday 16 December

Isaiah 39

'They have seen all that is in my house' (v.4)

The longing to be liked and accepted by others is a need that transcends generations. Natural as the desire might be, however, it can lead to actions and words that we later come to regret. This appears to be the chief concern of Isaiah when he questions Hezekiah after he has enthusiastically welcomed the Babylonian delegation – who are these men? Where have they come from? What have they seen? In his response, Isaiah highlights the rashness of Hezekiah's lack of discernment, and the future problems to which it would lead (vv.5-7).

The New Testament conveys a similar message: when Jesus sent his twelve disciples out on mission, he warned them that they would be like sheep among wolves, and that they would therefore need to 'be wise as serpents and innocent as doves' (Matthew 10.16). Discernment in their dealings with 'the world' would be vital.

We all need discernment in our dealings with others. For many, Facebook and other social media sites may well be a brilliant means of communication, but the lurid newspaper headlines resulting from people's over-exposure reveal the dark side of virtual communication only too clearly. Our faith urges us to love and reach out to all, but at the same time, Jesus warns us – his present-day disciples – to be careful how much of ourselves we disclose, and to whom. Otherwise we may, like Hezekiah, find that our rash judgements rebound on us in the future.

COLLECT

O Lord Jesus Christ,
who at your first coming sent your messenger
to prepare your way before you:
grant that the ministers and stewards of your mysteries
may likewise so prepare and make ready your way
by turning the hearts of the disobedient to the wisdom of the just,
that at your second coming to judge the world
we may be found an acceptable people in your sight;
for you are alive and reign with the Father
in the unity of the Holy Spirit,
one God, now and for ever.

Psalms **76**, 97 *or* 56, **57** (63*)
Zephaniah 1.1 – 2.3
Matthew 17.22-end

Thursday 17 December

Zephaniah 1.1 – 2.3

'Seek the Lord, all you humble of the land' (2.3)

The atmosphere darkens, and today's reading from Zephaniah makes grim reading. The day of the Lord is imminent, and the wrath and vengeance of God will be relentless. The universal destruction promised in the first few verses of chapter 1 is reminiscent of God's warning to Noah before the flood (Genesis 6.11-13). This time, the prophet warns that God will destroy all living creatures, with apparently no exceptions.

This message is not easy for us to hear today. What are we to make of all this distress and anguish, ruin and devastation, and how can we relate to it? The chief sin of the people seems to have been complacency, leading them to rely on the wealth and security they had acquired, rather than on God the generous giver (1.12). They have reduced God to an anaemic, powerless figurehead and will soon learn their mistake (1.13).

For Christians in the comfortable West, the danger of complacency in our faith is never far below the surface. We may wring our hands at the increasing secularization of society, but, so far at least, our right to be disciples of Christ has not been challenged. Even in times of economic downturn, many are so cushioned by their material possessions that they find it hard to express any actual *need* of God.

How acute is our need of God? And to what extent do we *really* consider ourselves accountable to him for the way we live?

God for whom we watch and wait,
you sent John the Baptist to prepare the way of your Son:
give us courage to speak the truth,
to hunger for justice,
and to suffer for the cause of right,
with Jesus Christ our Lord.

COLLECT

25

Friday 18 December

Zephaniah 3.1-13

'On that day you shall not be put to shame' (v.11)

Yesterday's warnings of general catastrophe become more specific. The city of Jerusalem itself is soiled and defiled; it has accepted no correction from God and has insisted on going her own way (vv.1-2). But then, unexpectedly, comes the promise of restoration. With the promise that the people 'will pasture and lie down' (v.13), we have moved from universal condemnation to 'the Lord is my shepherd' (Psalm 23) in a few short verses.

Our distance from the time in which this passage was written is vast, but the situation described has a depressingly familiar ring. Injustice and corruption are also rife today, not only in society at large, but also in the recent scandals that have bedevilled the Church. We are none of us immune; we share the common frailties of humanity and may often feel overwhelmed by the enormity of the scale of the darkness, both within and outside ourselves. Yet there is a promise here, restated with great reassurance, power and conviction at the beginning of John's Gospel. That promise is that, however bleak the situation may be, however impossible the possibility of healing and restoration may seem, the seeds of divine renewal lie buried within it. 'The light shines in the darkness, and the darkness did not overcome it' (John 1.5).

In what ways, and in what situations, might you be called upon to live this truth today?

COLLECT

O Lord Jesus Christ,
who at your first coming sent your messenger
to prepare your way before you:
grant that the ministers and stewards of your mysteries
may likewise so prepare and make ready your way
by turning the hearts of the disobedient to the wisdom of the just,
that at your second coming to judge the world
we may be found an acceptable people in your sight;
for you are alive and reign with the Father
in the unity of the Holy Spirit,
one God, now and for ever.

Zephaniah 3.14-end

'The Lord, your God, is in your midst' (v.17)

The momentum is now unstoppable, as the prophet urges the people to exultant praise. The nation and city are addressed as 'daughter' – her close kinship to the Lord unbreakable. His forgiveness of sin is reaffirmed and his protection assured (v.15). The day of the Lord ('On that day') is now promised as a time of irrepressible joy and freedom from fear (v.16). God himself will rejoice over his people, and renew them in his love (v.17).

The problem for believers, then and now, lies in the chasm between our present experience and the promise of future renewal and restoration. We look around and wonder how that chasm can ever be breached. Those who do find the light in the darkness often do so through a crisis, or a period of intense suffering: a severe illness, perhaps, or bereavement. People taken hostage face the daily threat of violent death, and live sometimes for years in isolation, cut off from familiar relationships and their normal daily routine.

This was the reality for Brian Keenan and his fellow Beirut hostages from 1986 to 1990. In *An Evil Cradling*, Keenan describes their surprise in discovering, in the dark heart of their captivity, a new and deeper freedom within themselves.

'The Lord, your God, is in your midst' (v.17). When we are in the midst of our own darkness, how can we reach out and connect with the same freedom and light within ourselves?

God for whom we watch and wait,
you sent John the Baptist to prepare the way of your Son:
give us courage to speak the truth,
to hunger for justice,
and to suffer for the cause of right,
with Jesus Christ our Lord.

COLLECT

27

Monday 21 December

Malachi 1.1, 6-end

'...where is the honour due to me?' (v.6)

It is difficult for us to identify a precise situation behind the attack in this passage against various cultic abuses. We may ask questions about possible economic and social causes, but such causes were not the prophet's principal focus. For Malachi, the failures in the cultic realm and the abysmal attitudes expressed in their performance were inextricably linked to the people's relationship to the divine. The earlier narrative about the boy Samuel, the priest Eli and his two faithless sons demonstrates the same correlation (1 Samuel 2–3).

This oracle is addressed to the 'priests who despise my name' (v.6). These priests have become lax and careless: polluted food has been offered, so polluting the altar on which it has been placed, and imperfect or sick animals have been offered for sacrifice. Even earthly masters would expect better than this, says Malachi, so how dare these priests think that such inferior service is good enough for God! 'I have no pleasure in you, says the Lord of hosts, and I will not accept an offering from your hands' (v.10).

There is a world-weariness in the priests' attitude; a tendency to take shortcuts and to think that any old thing will do (vv.13-14). But this specifically focused passage has an uncomfortably wide application. What about our own 'world-weariness'? What shortcuts do we take in our spiritual lives? And can we honestly say that we always offer God our best?

COLLECT

God our redeemer,
who prepared the Blessed Virgin Mary
to be the mother of your Son:
grant that, as she looked for his coming as our saviour,
so we may be ready to greet him
when he comes again as our judge;
who is alive and reigns with you,
in the unity of the Holy Spirit,
one God, now and for ever.

Malachi 2.1-16

'And what does the one God desire? Godly offspring.' (v.15)

The diatribe against Israel's priests continues. If they will not listen and give glory to God's name, then their blessings will rebound on them as curses (v.2). Their children also will be afflicted, and there is a strong echo here of the vow that God made to Israel through Moses on Mount Sinai: that the sins of the parents would be visited 'upon the children … to the third and the fourth generation' (Exodus 34.7).

One of the sins these priests stand accused of is complacency, and again, we need to be careful we don't fall into the same trap. I once heard of a most effective sermon relating to Jesus' parable of the Pharisee and the tax-collector (Luke 18.9-14). It consisted of precisely thirteen words: 'Hands up anyone who didn't think, "Thank God I'm not like that Pharisee!"' Think carefully about this for a minute, and you will see we are caught whether we raise our hands or not! Ouch.

The situation may be specific, but the message is universally applicable. Not only priests are called to be 'Godly offspring' (v.15). All of us are called to truly revere and worship God; all are likewise called to walk with God 'in integrity and uprightness' (v.6). We are frail humans, so often blind to our true motives and desires. Our walk with God calls for honest self-examination: 'So take heed to yourselves' says Malachi, 'and do not be faithless' (v.16).

Eternal God,
as Mary waited for the birth of your Son,
so we wait for his coming in glory;
bring us through the birth pangs of this present age
to see, with her, our great salvation
in Jesus Christ our Lord.

COLLECT

Wednesday 23 December

Malachi 2.17 – 3.12

'You have wearied the Lord with your words' (2.17)

Malachi continues to build up a picture of wrongdoing that the perpetrators seek to justify – to themselves, to others and to God. God will have no more of such duplicity, and a messenger will be sent to prepare his way. The identity of the messenger is not specified here (in 3.1, although 4.5 is more specific). By the time of the New Testament, the synoptic gospels clearly identify the unnamed messenger with John the Baptist (Matthew 11.10; Luke 7.27; Mark 1.2).

And now, the thrust of Malachi's message begins to shift. Sin is still abhorrent, but the Lord's call through the prophet is a plea for a renewal of trust. It speaks to us today as it did to Israel: 'Return to me, and I will return to you' (3.7). What follows is a ringing affirmation of God's constant love for his people, as expressed in Malachi 1.2, and his longing to provide abundantly for all their needs. If they return to a position of basic trust, then they 'will be a land of delight, says the Lord of hosts' (3.12).

In today's complex world it isn't always easy for us to draw the line between responsible provision for future needs and the sort of open-hearted abandon that seems to be advocated here. But hopefully and prayerfully such discernment is possible, if we are able to see ourselves as stewards with gifts to be shared rather than owners with possessions to be hoarded.

COLLECT

God our redeemer,
who prepared the Blessed Virgin Mary
to be the mother of your Son:
grant that, as she looked for his coming as our saviour,
so we may be ready to greet him
when he comes again as our judge;
who is alive and reigns with you,
in the unity of the Holy Spirit,
one God, now and for ever.

Thursday 24 December

Christmas Eve

Malachi 3.13 – end of 4

'They shall be mine, says the Lord of hosts' (3.17)

The message continues its new trajectory from darkness towards light. The arrogant continue to question what gain there could possibly be in serving the Lord. At the same time they are set against those who revere God, those whom God claims for his possession (3.17-18). For those who despise and reject God, the day of the Lord will bring terrible judgement, but for those who revere his name 'the sun of righteousness shall rise, with healing in its wings' (4.2).

Gathering up the threads of his message, the prophet directs his hearers to the wisdom of the past. The people are urged to remember the teaching of Moses, and the anonymous messenger from Chapter 3 (see yesterday's reflection) is here named as Elijah (4.5). Jesus himself makes the connection between these two references and John the Baptist (Matthew 11.10-14).

So, as we stand on the very threshold of Christ's birth, the prophecy of Malachi points to the messengers who prepare the way for him. In Christian tradition, of course, the ultimate 'messenger' is Jesus himself, the one in whom the kingdom of God has come among us (Matthew 12.28).

Some commentators have felt that the ambiguity of the messenger's identity is a weakness in Malachi's message, but that very ambiguity can spur us to deeper levels of 'seeing' and discernment. Who – and where – are the 'messengers of the covenant' today? And would all Christians agree on who they are?

COLLECT

Almighty God,
you make us glad with the yearly remembrance
of the birth of your Son Jesus Christ:
grant that, as we joyfully receive him as our redeemer,
so we may with sure confidence behold him
when he shall come to be our judge;
who is alive and reigns with you,
in the unity of the Holy Spirit,
one God, now and for ever.

Morning Prayer – a simple form

Preparation

O Lord, open our lips
and our mouth shall proclaim your praise.

A prayer of thanksgiving for Advent

Blessed are you, Sovereign God of all,
to you be praise and glory for ever.
In your tender compassion
the dawn from on high is breaking upon us
to dispel the lingering shadows of night.
As we look for your coming among us this day,
open our eyes to behold your presence
and strengthen our hands to do your will,
that the world may rejoice and give you praise.
Blessed be God, Father, Son and Holy Spirit.
Blessed be God for ever.

Word of God

Psalmody *(the psalm or psalms listed for the day)*

**Glory to the Father and to the Son
and to the Holy Spirit;
as it was in the beginning is now:
and shall be for ever. Amen.**

Reading from Holy Scripture *(one or both of the passages set for the day)*

Reflection

The Benedictus (The Song of Zechariah) *(see opposite page)*

Prayers

Intercessions – a time of prayer for the day and its tasks, the world and its need, the church and her life.

The Collect for the Day

The Lord's Prayer *(see p. 35)*

Conclusion

A blessing or the Grace *(see p. 35)*, or a concluding response

Let us bless the Lord
Thanks be to God

Benedictus (The Song of Zechariah)

1. Blessed be the Lord the God of Israel, ♦
   who has come to his people and set them free.

2. He has raised up for us a mighty Saviour, ♦
   born of the house of his servant David.

3. Through his holy prophets God promised of old ♦
   to save us from our enemies,
   from the hands of all that hate us,

4. To show mercy to our ancestors, ♦
   and to remember his holy covenant.

5. This was the oath God swore to our father Abraham: ♦
   to set us free from the hands of our enemies,

6. Free to worship him without fear, ♦
   holy and righteous in his sight
   all the days of our life.

7. And you, child, shall be called the prophet of the Most High, ♦
   for you will go before the Lord to prepare his way,

8. To give his people knowledge of salvation ♦
   by the forgiveness of all their sins.

9. In the tender compassion of our God ♦
   the dawn from on high shall break upon us,

10. To shine on those who dwell in darkness
    and the shadow of death, ♦
    and to guide our feet into the way of peace.

Luke 1.68-79

**Glory to the Father and to the Son
and to the Holy Spirit;
as it was in the beginning is now:
and shall be for ever. Amen.**

Seasonal Prayers of Thanksgiving

Advent

Blessed are you, Sovereign God of all,
to you be praise and glory for ever.
In your tender compassion
the dawn from on high is breaking upon us
to dispel the lingering shadows of night.
As we look for your coming among us this day,
open our eyes to behold your presence
and strengthen our hands to do your will,
that the world may rejoice and give you praise.
Blessed be God, Father, Son and Holy Spirit.
Blessed be God for ever.

At Any Time

Blessed are you, creator of all,
to you be praise and glory for ever.
As your dawn renews the face of the earth
bringing light and life to all creation,
may we rejoice in this day you have made;
as we wake refreshed from the depths of sleep,
open our eyes to behold your presence
and strengthen our hands to do your will,
that the world may rejoice and give you praise.
Blessed be God, Father, Son and Holy Spirit.
Blessed be God for ever.

after Lancelot Andrewes (1626)

The Lord's Prayer and The Grace

Our Father in heaven,
hallowed be your name,
your kingdom come,
your will be done,
on earth as in heaven.
Give us today our daily bread.
Forgive us our sins
as we forgive those who sin against us.
Lead us not into temptation
but deliver us from evil.
For the kingdom, the power,
and the glory are yours
now and for ever.
Amen.

(or)

Our Father, who art in heaven,
hallowed be thy name;
thy kingdom come;
thy will be done;
on earth as it is in heaven.
Give us this day our daily bread.
And forgive us our trespasses,
as we forgive those who trespass against us.
And lead us not into temptation;
but deliver us from evil.
For thine is the kingdom,
the power and the glory,
for ever and ever.
Amen.

The grace of our Lord Jesus Christ,
and the love of God,
and the fellowship of the Holy Spirit,
be with us all evermore.
Amen.

An Order for Night Prayer (Compline)

The Lord almighty grant us a quiet night and a perfect end.
Amen.

Our help is in the name of the Lord
who made heaven and earth.

A period of silence for reflection on the past day may follow.

The following or other suitable words of penitence may be used

Most merciful God,
we confess to you,
before the whole company of heaven and one another,
that we have sinned in thought, word and deed
and in what we have failed to do.
Forgive us our sins,
heal us by your Spirit
and raise us to new life in Christ. Amen.

O God, make speed to save us.
O Lord, make haste to help us.

Glory to the Father and to the Son
and to the Holy Spirit;
as it was in the beginning is now
and shall be for ever. Amen.
Alleluia.

The following or another suitable hymn may be sung

Before the ending of the day,
Creator of the world, we pray
That you, with steadfast love, would keep
Your watch around us while we sleep.

From evil dreams defend our sight,
From fears and terrors of the night;
Tread underfoot our deadly foe
That we no sinful thought may know.

O Father, that we ask be done
Through Jesus Christ, your only Son;
And Holy Spirit, by whose breath
Our souls are raised to life from death.

The Word of God

Psalmody

One or more of Psalms 4, 91 or 134 may be used.

Psalm 134

1   Come, bless the Lord, all you servants of the Lord, ♦
you that by night stand in the house of the Lord.

2   Lift up your hands towards the sanctuary ♦
and bless the Lord.

3   The Lord who made heaven and earth ♦
give you blessing out of Zion.

**Glory to the Father and to the Son
and to the Holy Spirit;
as it was in the beginning is now
and shall be for ever. Amen.**

Scripture Reading

*One of the following short lessons or another suitable
passage is read*

You, O Lord, are in the midst of us and we are called by your
name; leave us not, O Lord our God.

Jeremiah 14.9

(or)

Be sober, be vigilant, because your adversary the devil is
prowling round like a roaring lion, seeking for someone
to devour. Resist him, strong in the faith.

1 Peter 5.8,9

(or)

The servants of the Lamb shall see the face of God, whose name
will be on their foreheads. There will be no more night: they will
not need the light of a lamp or the light of the sun, for God will
be their light, and they will reign for ever and ever.

Revelation 22.4,5

Into your hands, O Lord, I commend my spirit.
Into your hands, O Lord, I commend my spirit.
For you have redeemed me, Lord God of truth.
I commend my spirit.
Glory to the Father and to the Son
and to the Holy Spirit.
Into your hands, O Lord, I commend my spirit.

Or, in Easter

Into your hands, O Lord, I commend my spirit.
   Alleluia, alleluia.
Into your hands, O Lord, I commend my spirit.
   Alleluia, alleluia.
For you have redeemed me, Lord God of truth.
Alleluia, alleluia.
Glory to the Father and to the Son
and to the Holy Spirit.
Into your hands, O Lord, I commend my spirit.
   Alleluia, alleluia.

Keep me as the apple of your eye.
Hide me under the shadow of your wings.

Gospel Canticle

Nunc Dimittis (The Song of Simeon)

**Save us, O Lord, while waking,
and guard us while sleeping,
that awake we may watch with Christ
and asleep may rest in peace.**

1   Now, Lord, you let your servant go in peace:
    your word has been fulfilled.

2   My own eyes have seen the salvation
    which you have prepared in the sight of every people;

3   A light to reveal you to the nations
    and the glory of your people Israel.

Luke 2.29-32

**Glory to the Father and to the Son
and to the Holy Spirit;
as it was in the beginning is now
and shall be for ever. Amen.**

**Save us, O Lord, while waking,
and guard us while sleeping,
that awake we may watch with Christ
and asleep may rest in peace.**

Prayers

Intercessions and thanksgivings may be offered here.

The Collect

Visit this place, O Lord, we pray,
and drive far from it the snares of the enemy;
may your holy angels dwell with us and guard us in peace,
and may your blessing be always upon us;
through Jesus Christ our Lord.
Amen.

The Lord's Prayer (see p. 35) may be said.

The Conclusion

In peace we will lie down and sleep;
for you alone, Lord, make us dwell in safety.

Abide with us, Lord Jesus,
for the night is at hand and the day is now past.

As the night watch looks for the morning,
so do we look for you, O Christ.

[Come with the dawning of the day
and make yourself known in the breaking of the bread.]

The Lord bless us and watch over us;
the Lord make his face shine upon us and be gracious to us;
the Lord look kindly on us and give us peace.
Amen.

Love what you've read?

Why not consider using
Reflections for Daily Prayer
all year round? We also publish
these Bible reflections in an
annual format, containing
material for the entire
church year.

The volume for the **2015/16**
church year is now available
and features contributions from
a host of distinguished writers:
Rosalind Brown, Gillian Cooper,
Steven Croft, Andrew Davison,
Maggi Dawn, Paula Gooder,
Peter Graystone, Mary Gregory,
Malcolm Guite, Emma Ineson, Jan McFarlane,
Barbara Mosse, Mark Oakley, Martyn Percy, Ben Quash,
Martyn Snow and Jane Williams.

Reflections for Daily Prayer:
Advent 2015 to the eve of Advent 2016
ISBN 978 0 7151 4457 2 • **£16.99**

**Please note this book reproduces the material for Advent
found in the volume you are now holding.**

Reflections for Daily Prayer **2016/17** will be
available from May 2016 with reflections written by:
Jeff Astley, Joanna Collicutt, Jonathan Frost,
Paula Gooder, Steven Croft, Helen-Ann Hartley,
Libby Lane, Graham Jones, Helen Orchard,
John Perumbalath, Sarah Rowland Jones, Tim Sledge,
Angela Tilby and Margaret Whipp.

Reflections for Daily Prayer:
Advent 2016 to the eve of Advent 2017
ISBN 978 0 7151 4715 3
£16.99 • 336 pages

Reflections for Daily Prayer
App

Make Bible study and reflection a part of your routine wherever you go with the Reflections for Daily Prayer App for Apple and Android devices.

Download the app for free from the App Store (Apple devices) or Google Play (Android devices) and receive a week's worth of reflections free. Then purchase a monthly, three-monthly or annual subscription to receive up-to-date content.

Reflections on the Psalms

£14.99 • 192 pages
ISBN 978 0 7151 4490 9

Reflections on the Psalms provides original and insightful meditations on each of the Bible's 150 Psalms, from the same experienced team of writers that have made *Reflections for Daily Prayer* so successful.

Each reflection is accompanied by its corresponding Psalm refrain and prayer from the *Common Worship Psalter*, making this a valuable resource for personal or devotional use. Specially written introductions by Paula Gooder and Steven Croft explore the Psalms and the Bible and the Psalms in the life of the Church.

Also available in Kindle and epub formats

Reflections for Lent 2016

Wednesday 10 February – Saturday 26 March 2016

This shortened edition of *Reflections* is ideal for group or church use during Lent, or for anyone seeking a daily devotional guide to this most holy season of the Christian year. It is also ideal as a taster for those wanting to begin a regular pattern of prayer and reading.

Authors:
Paula Gooder, Andrew Davison, Martyn Percy and Steven Croft

£4.99 • 48 pages
ISBN 978 0 7151 4709 2
Available November 2015

Resources for Daily Prayer

Common Worship: Daily Prayer

The official daily office of the Church of England,
Common Worship: Daily Prayer is a rich collection
of devotional material that will enable those
wanting to enrich their quiet times to develop
a regular pattern of prayer. It includes:

- Prayer During the Day
- Forms of Penitence
- Morning and Evening Prayer
- Night Prayer (Compline)
- Collects and Refrains
- Canticles
- Complete Psalter

896 pages • with 6 ribbons • 202 x 125mm

Hardback	978 0 7151 2199 3	£22.50
Soft cased	978 0 7151 2178 8	£27.50
Bonded leather	978 0 7151 2277 8	£50.00

Time to Pray

This compact, soft-case volume offers two simple, shorter
offices from *Common Worship: Daily Prayer*.
It is an ideal introduction to a more structured personal
devotional time, or can be used as a lighter, portable
daily office for those on the move.

Time to Pray includes:

- Prayer During the Day
  (for every day of the week)
- Night Prayer
- Selected Psalms

£12.99 • 112 pages • Soft case
ISBN 978 0 7151 2122 1

Order now at www.chpublishing.co.uk
or via **Norwich Books and Music**
Telephone **(01603) 785923**
E-mail **orders@norwichbooksandmusic.co.uk**